Coloring book for adults and kids amazing ass image for design

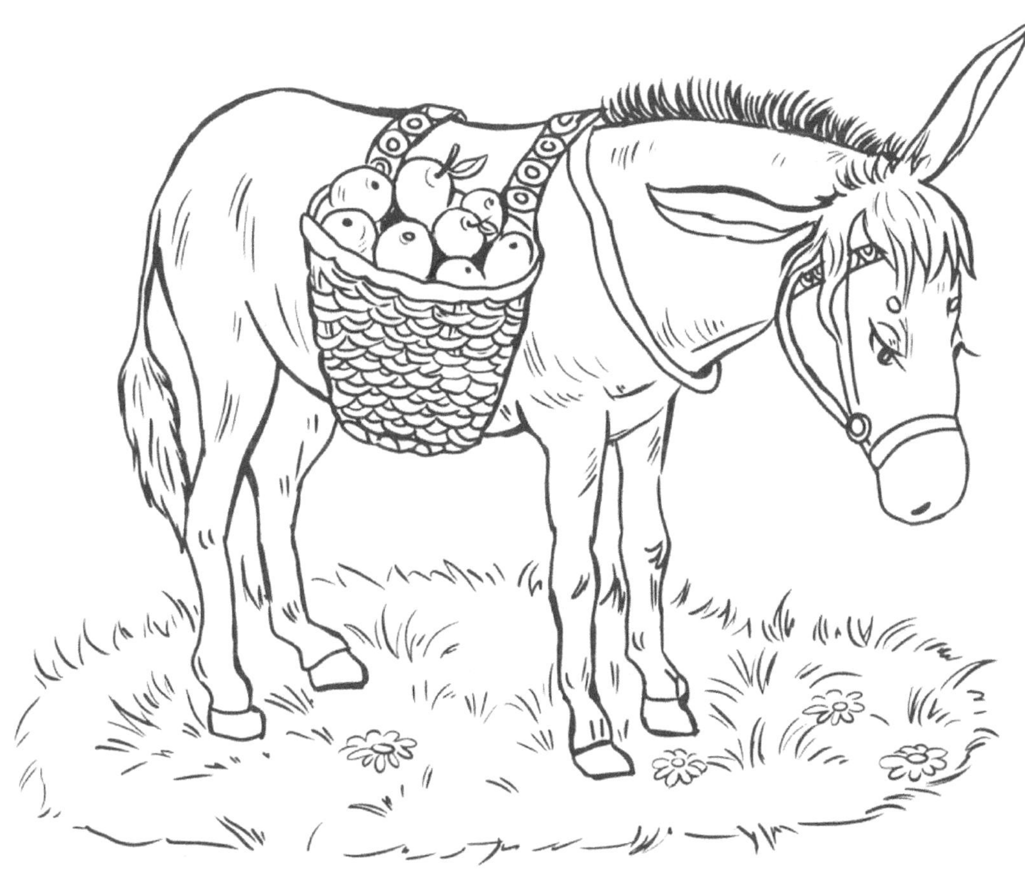

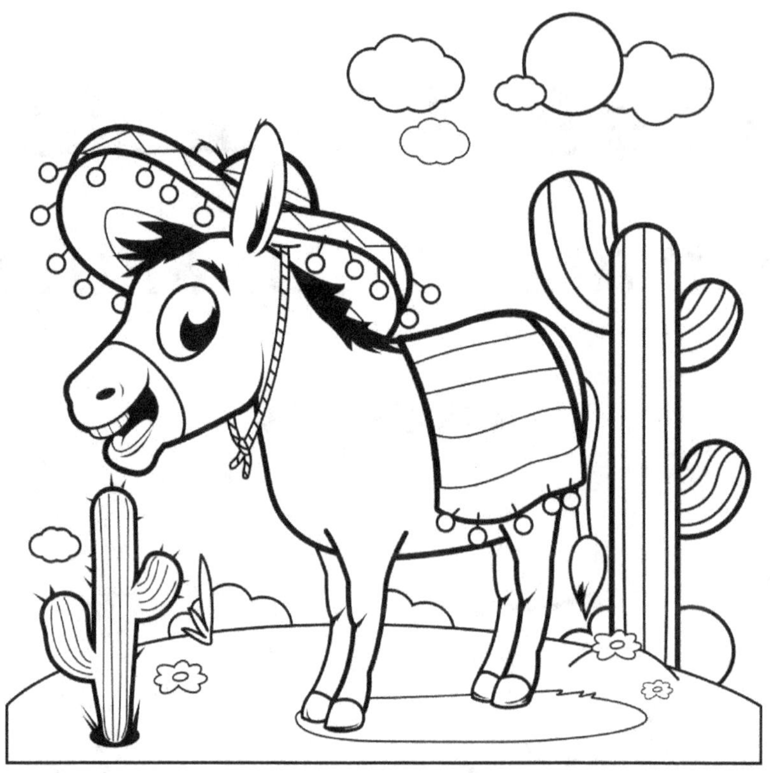

This coloring book is belongs to

____

____

____

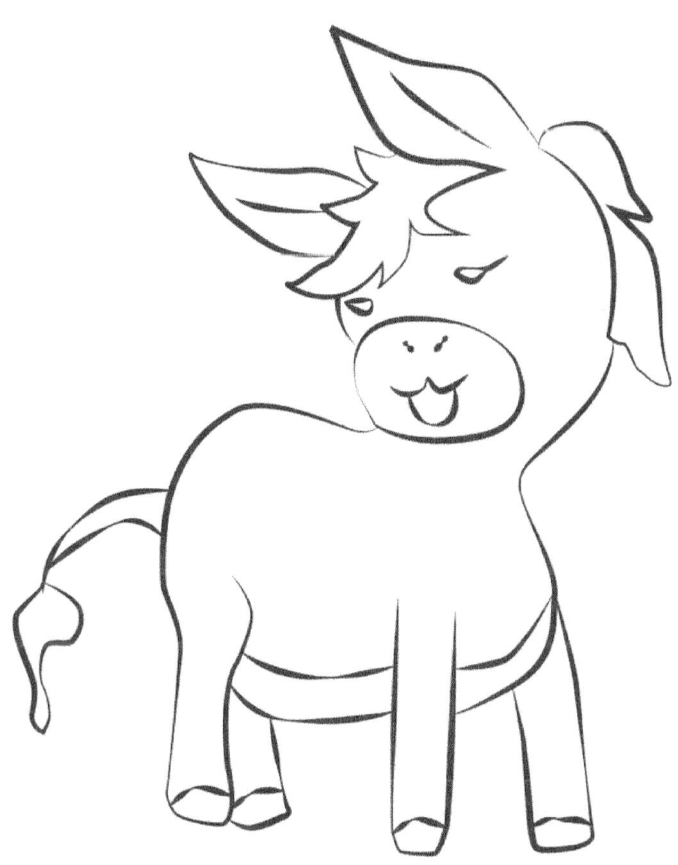

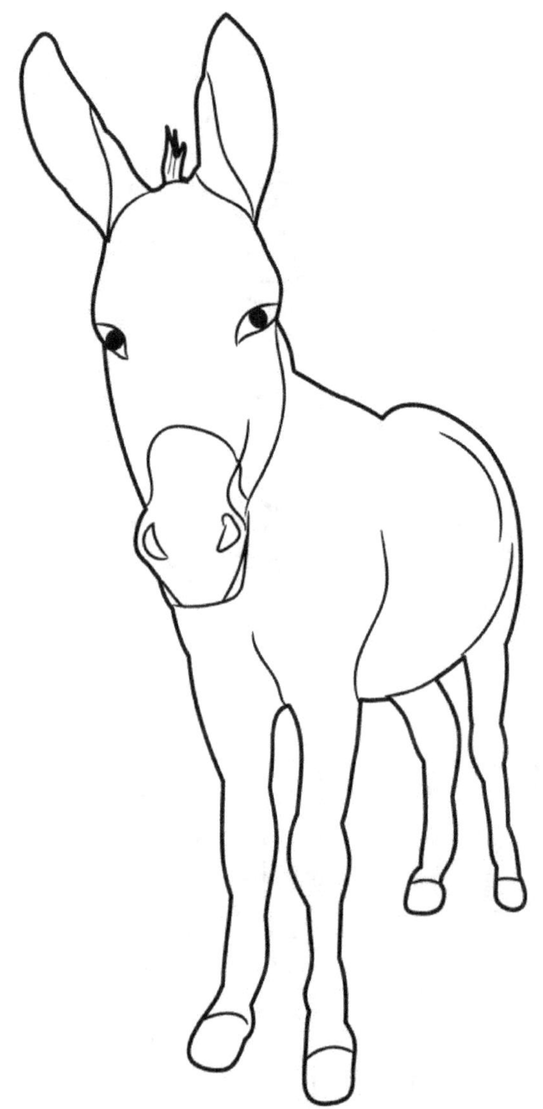

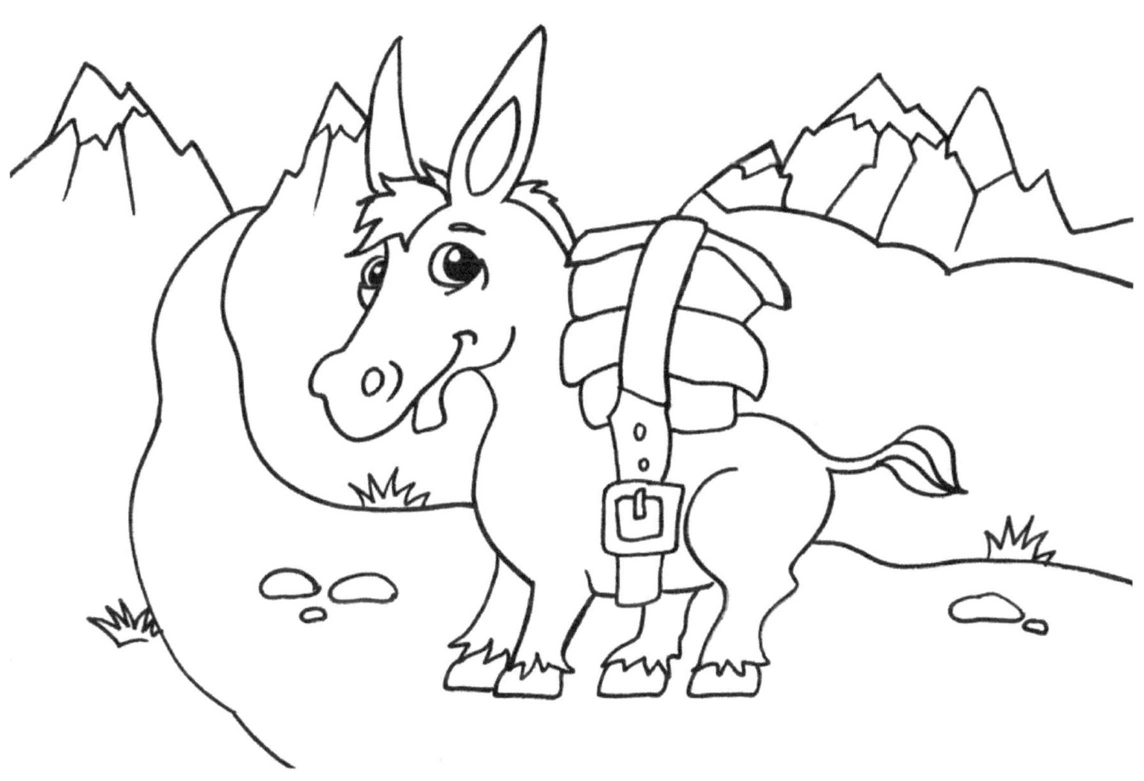

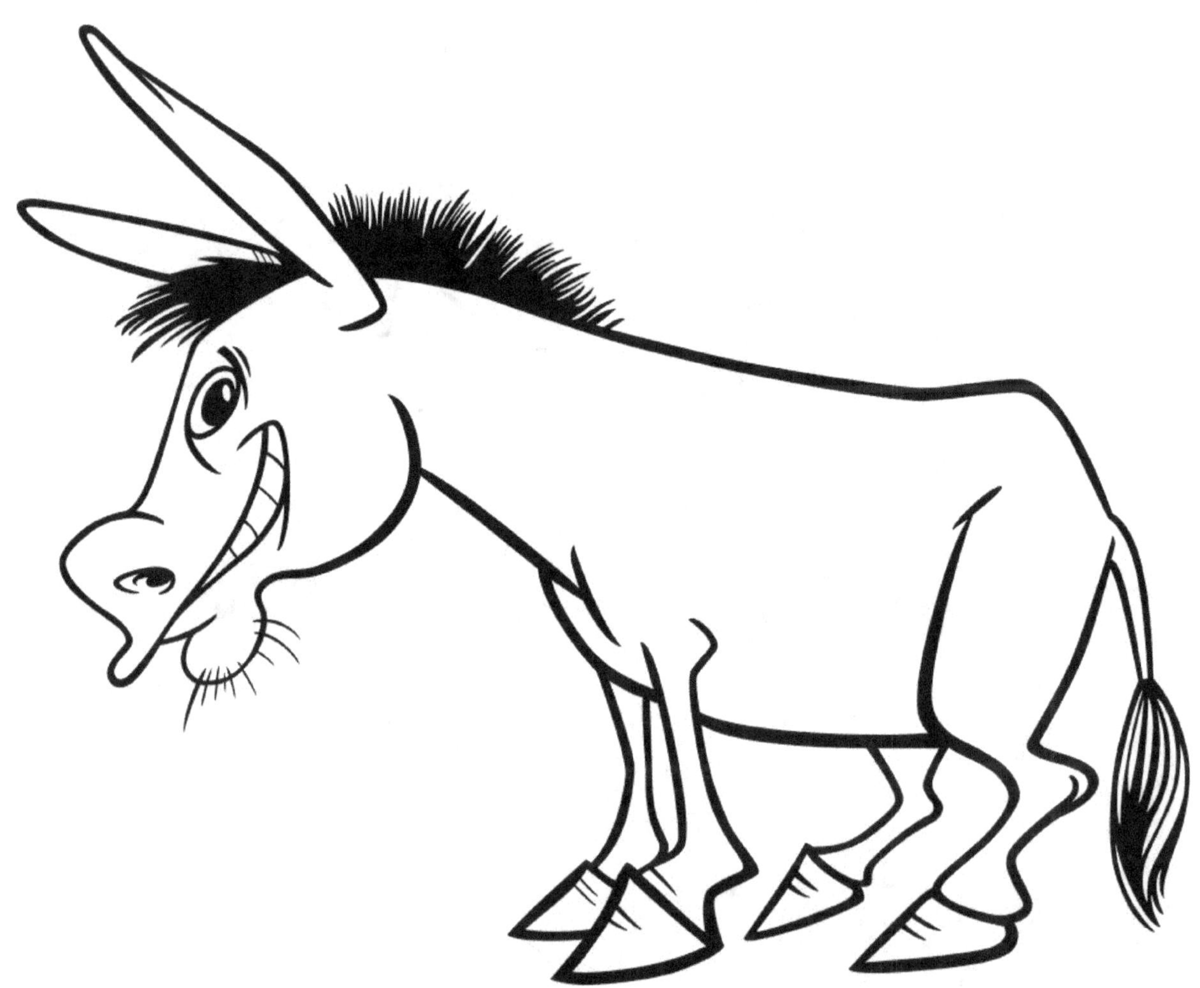

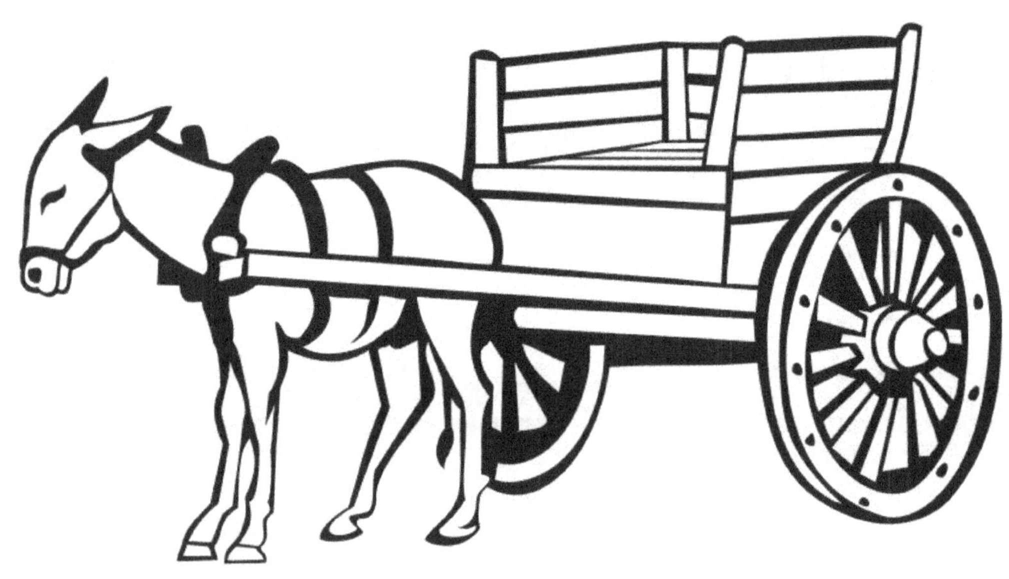

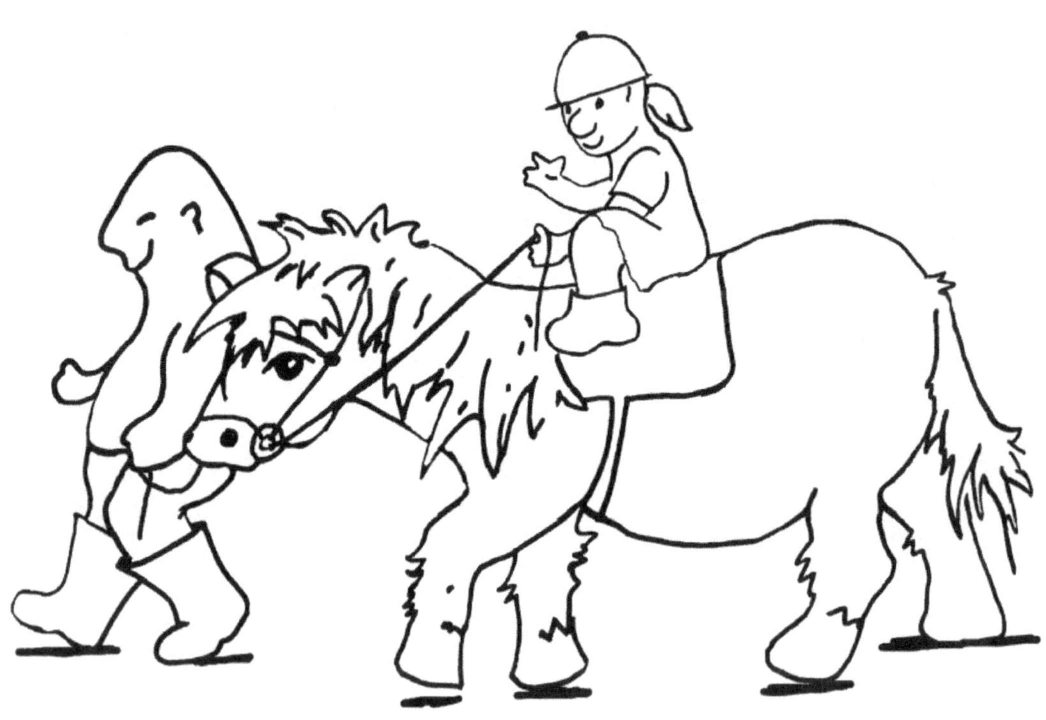

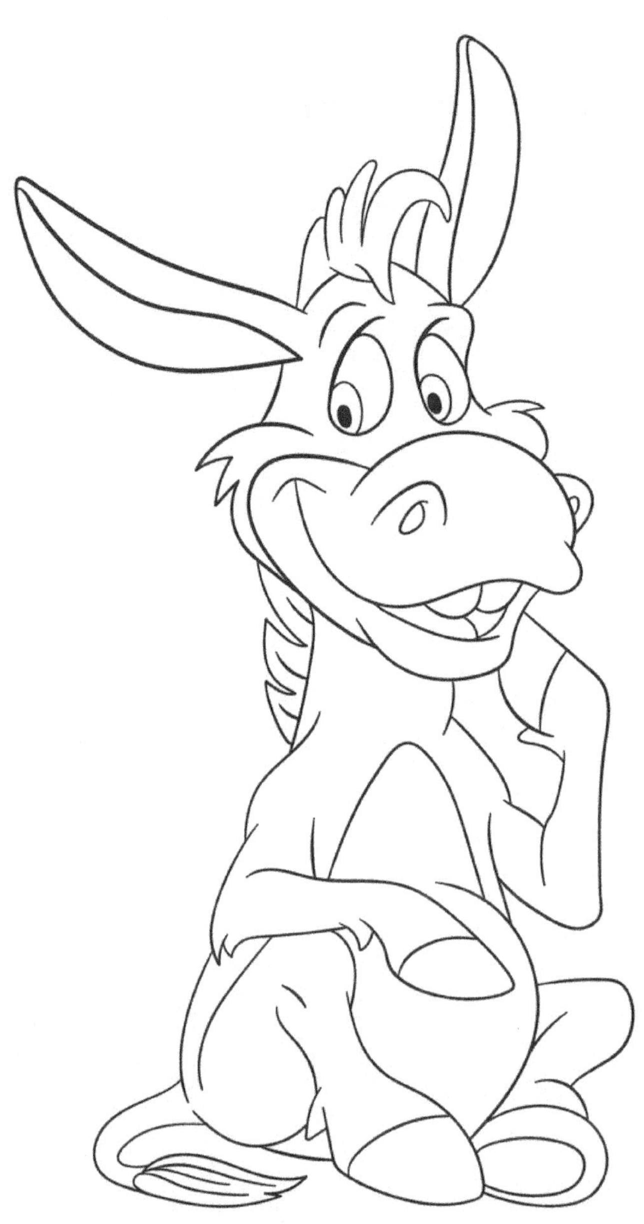

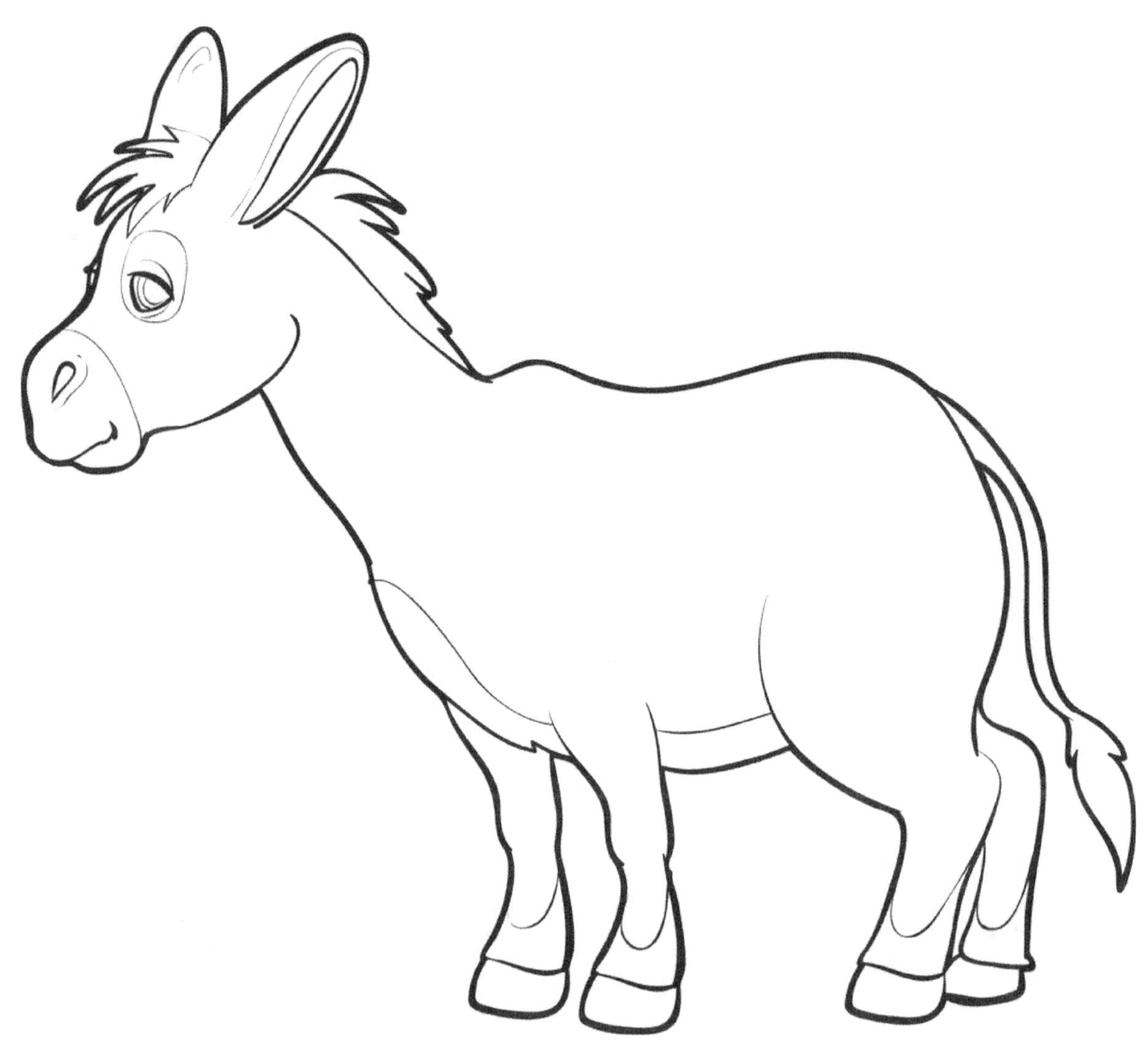

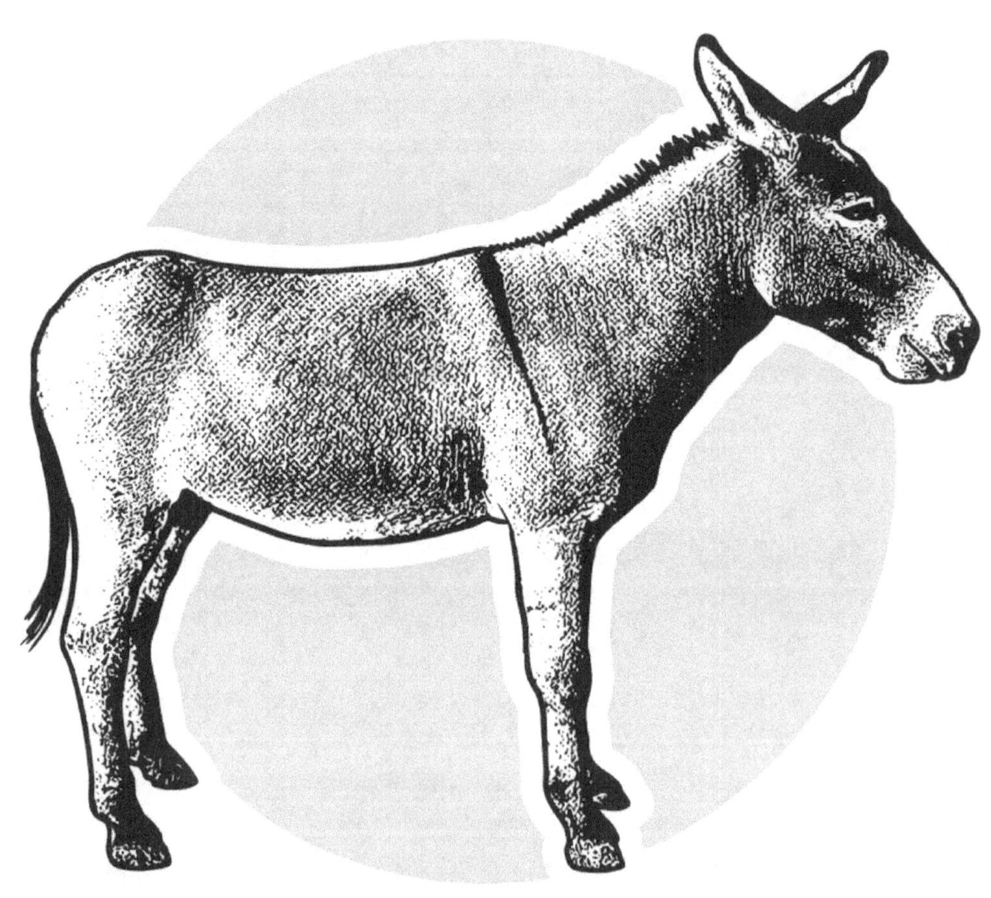

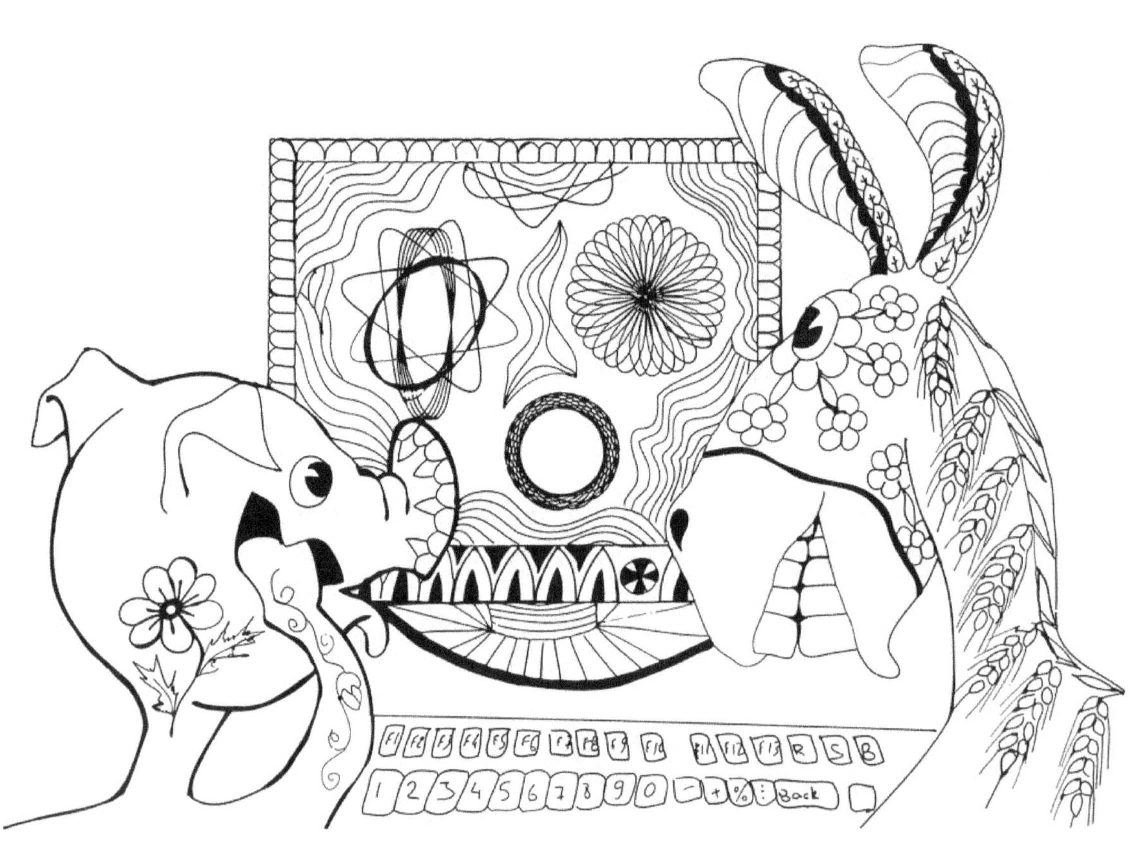

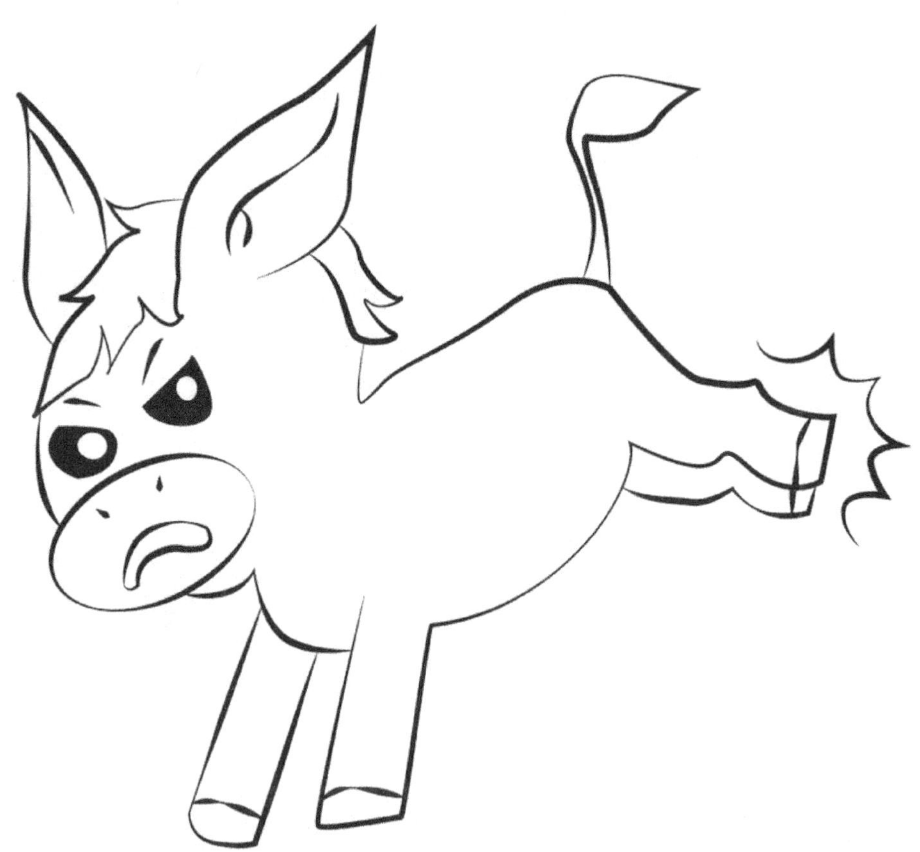

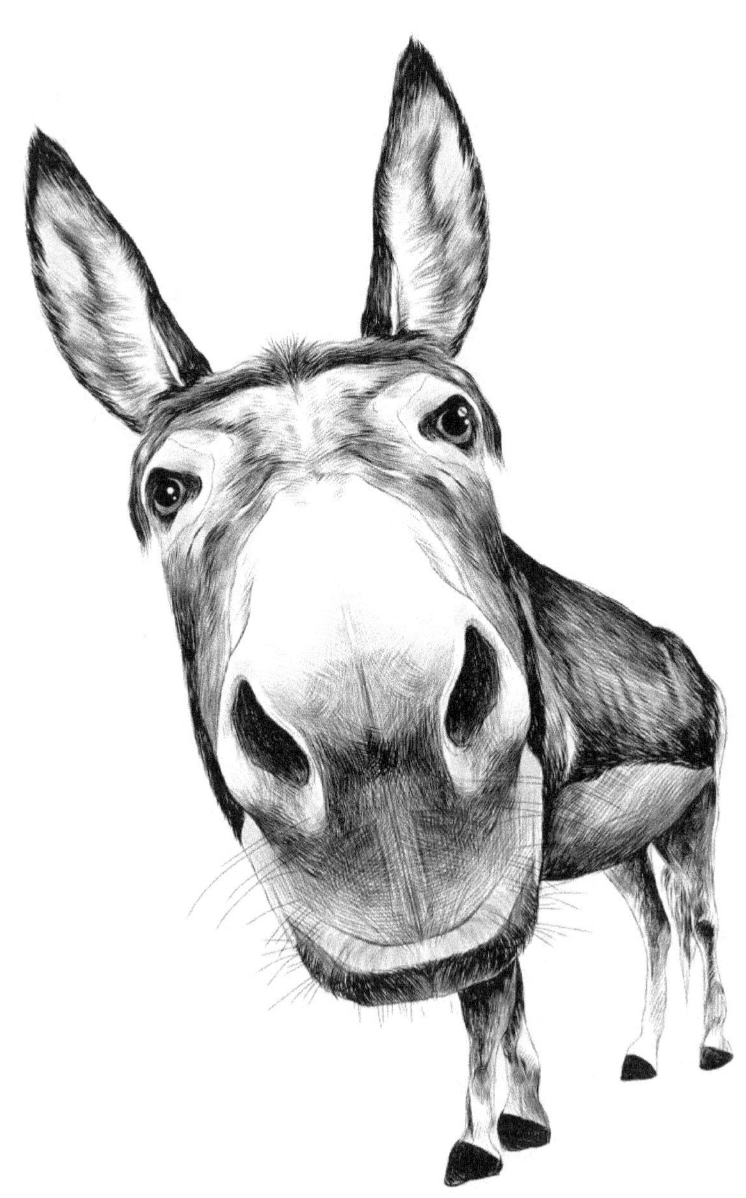

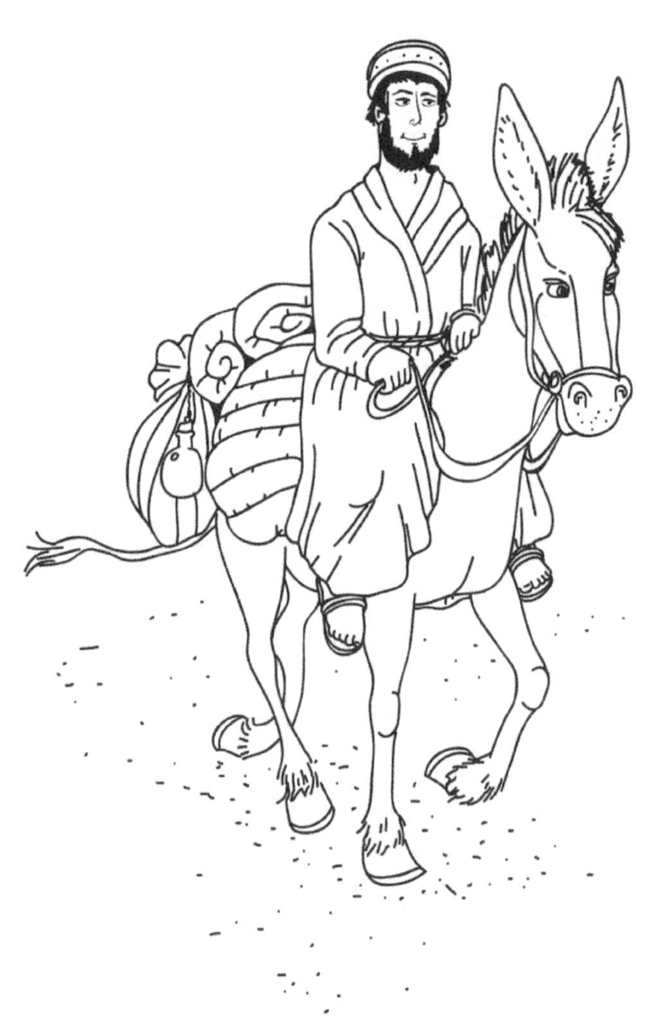

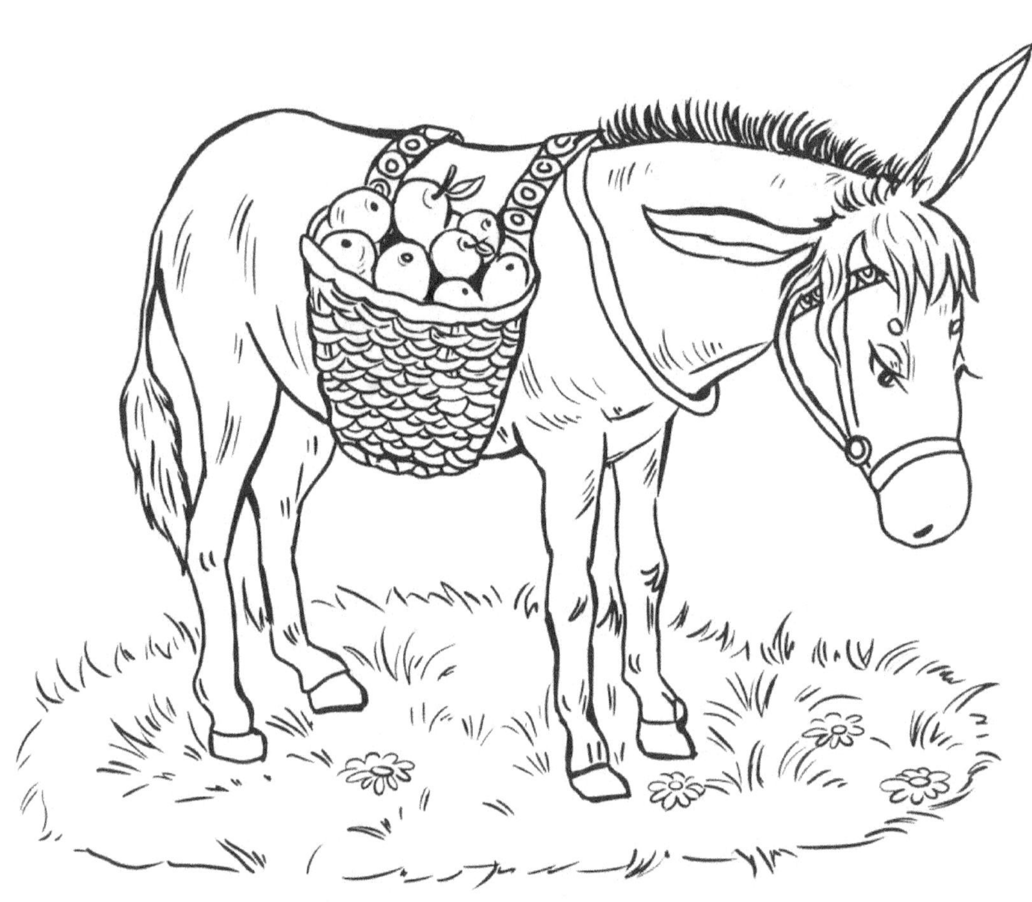

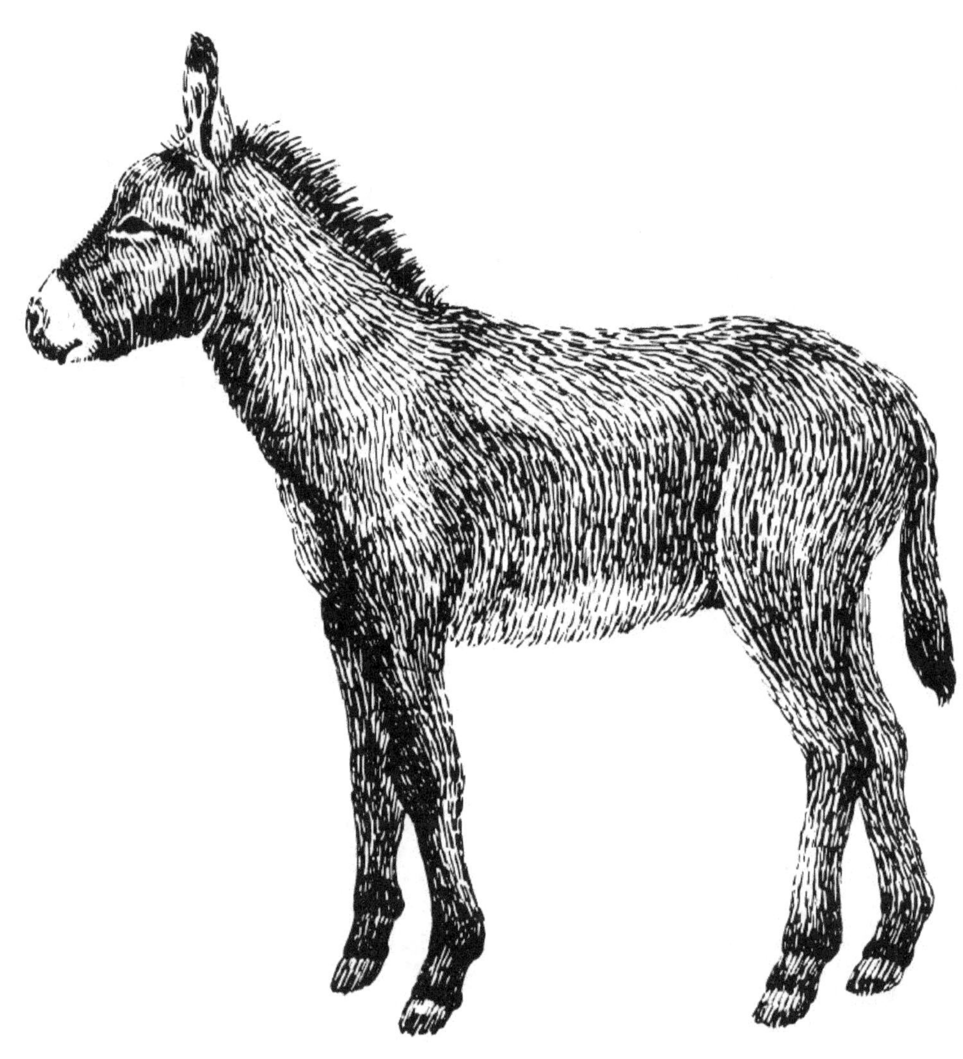

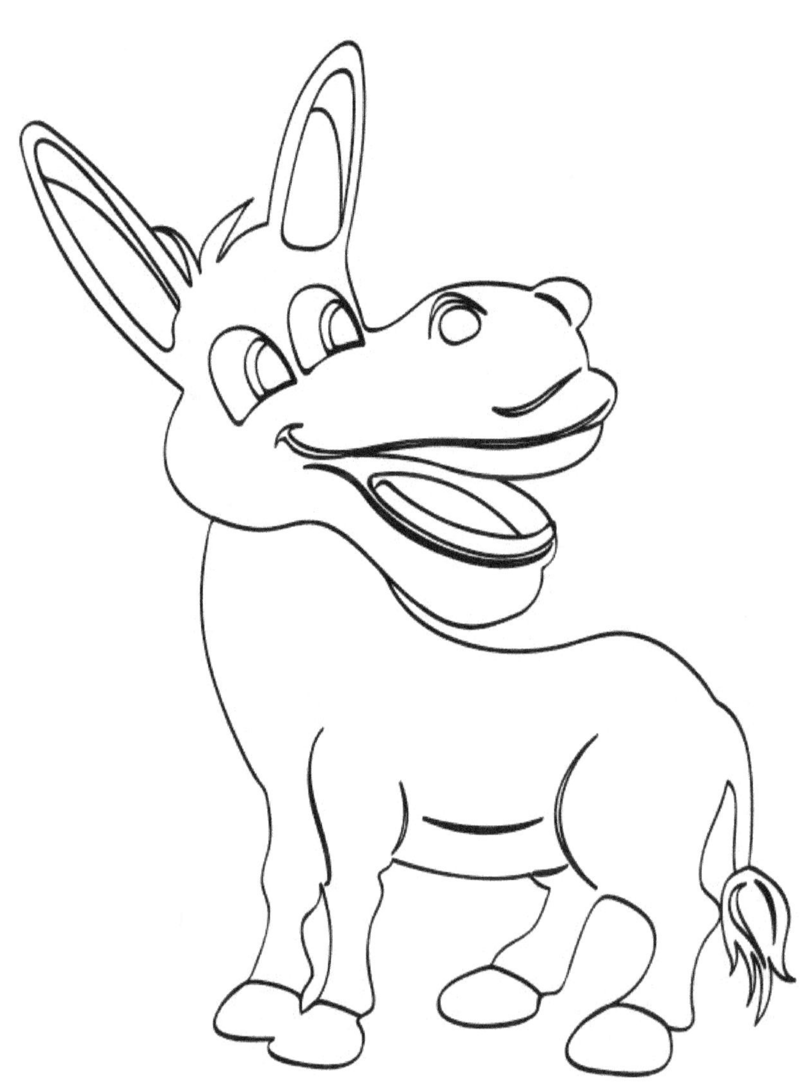

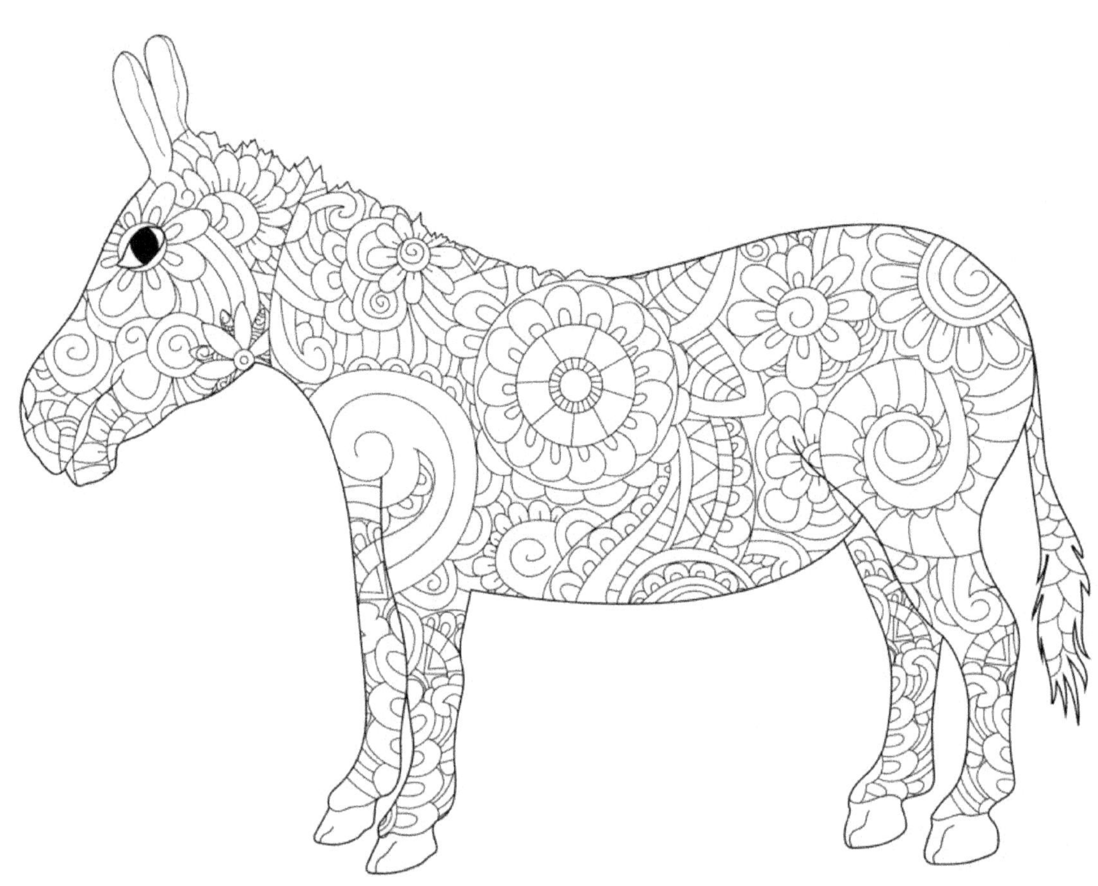

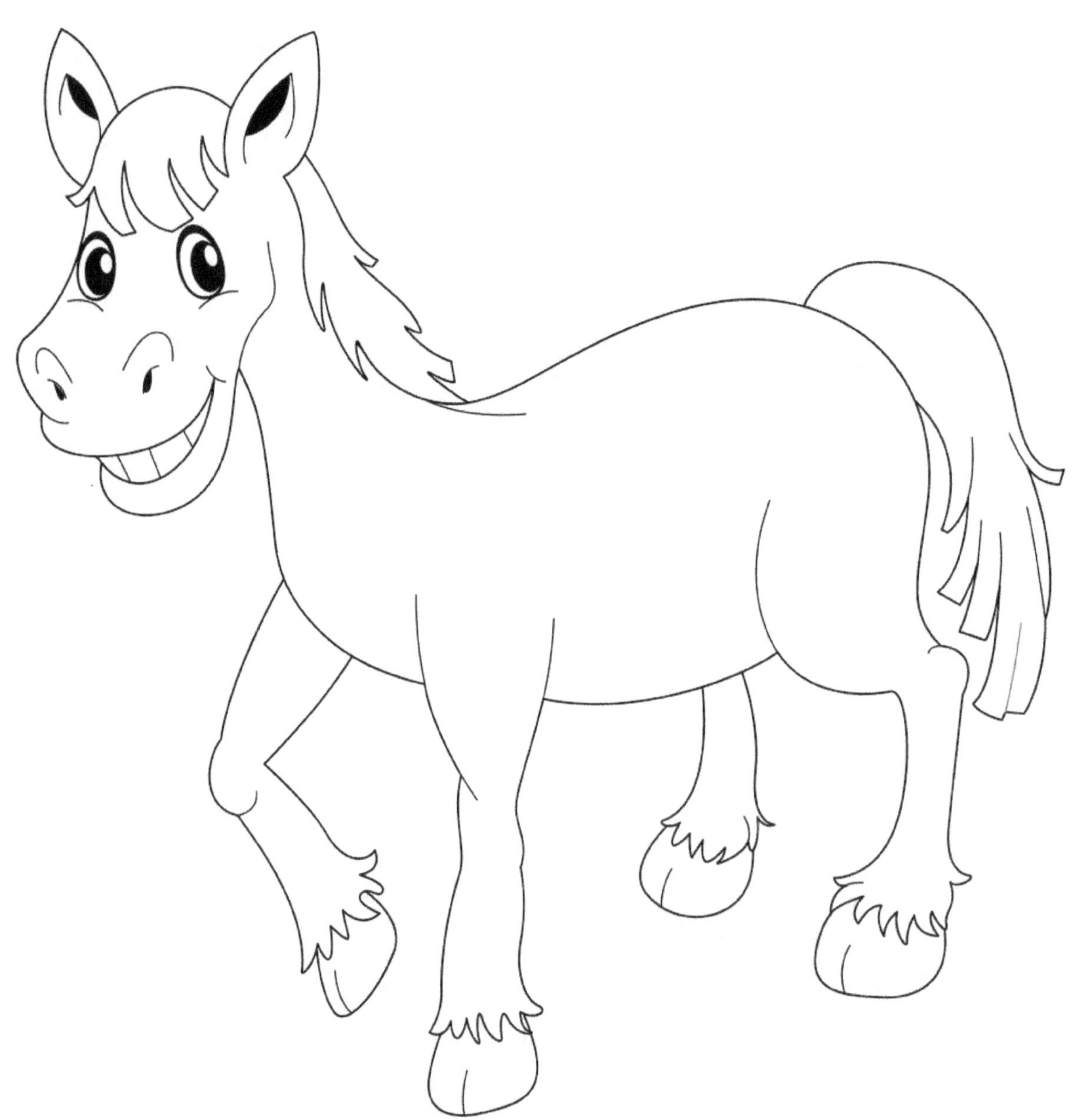

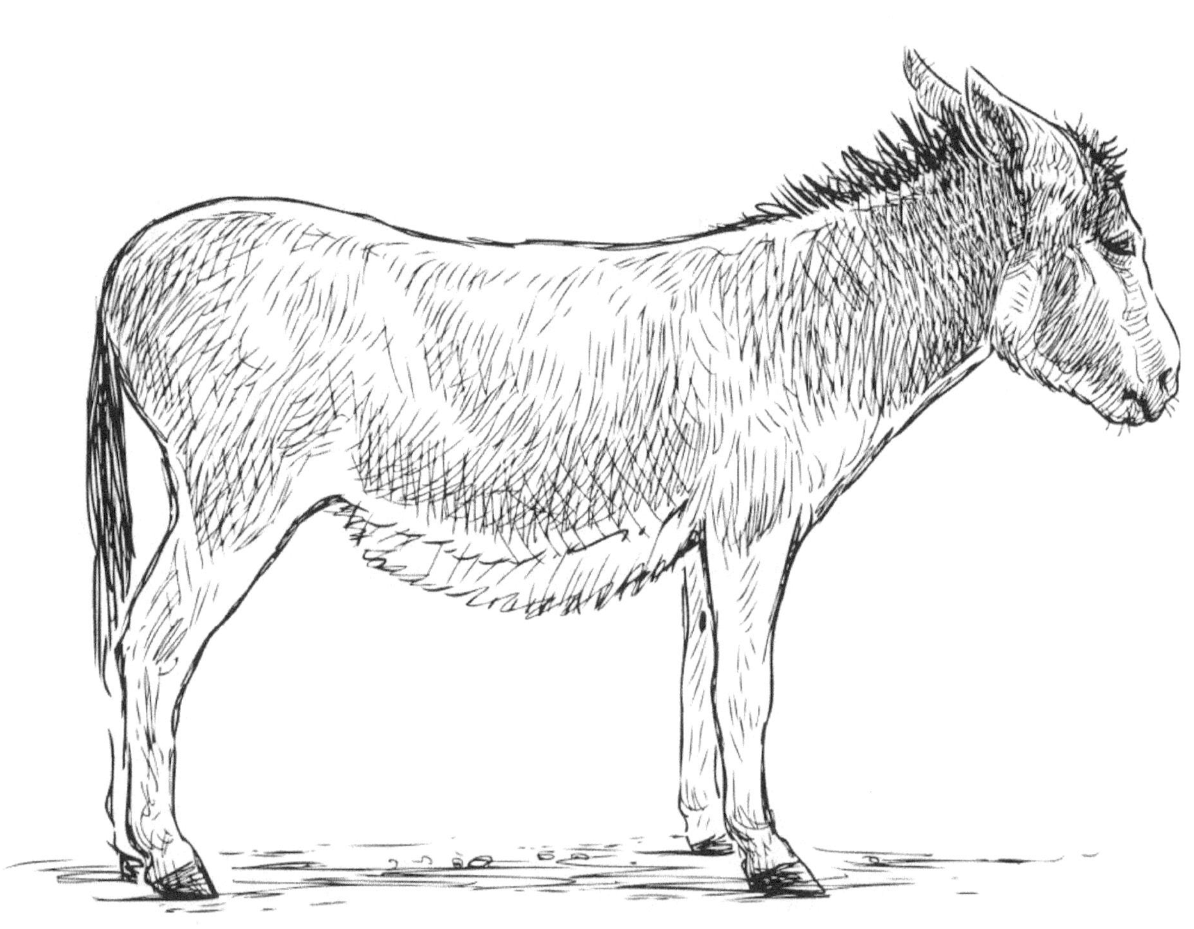

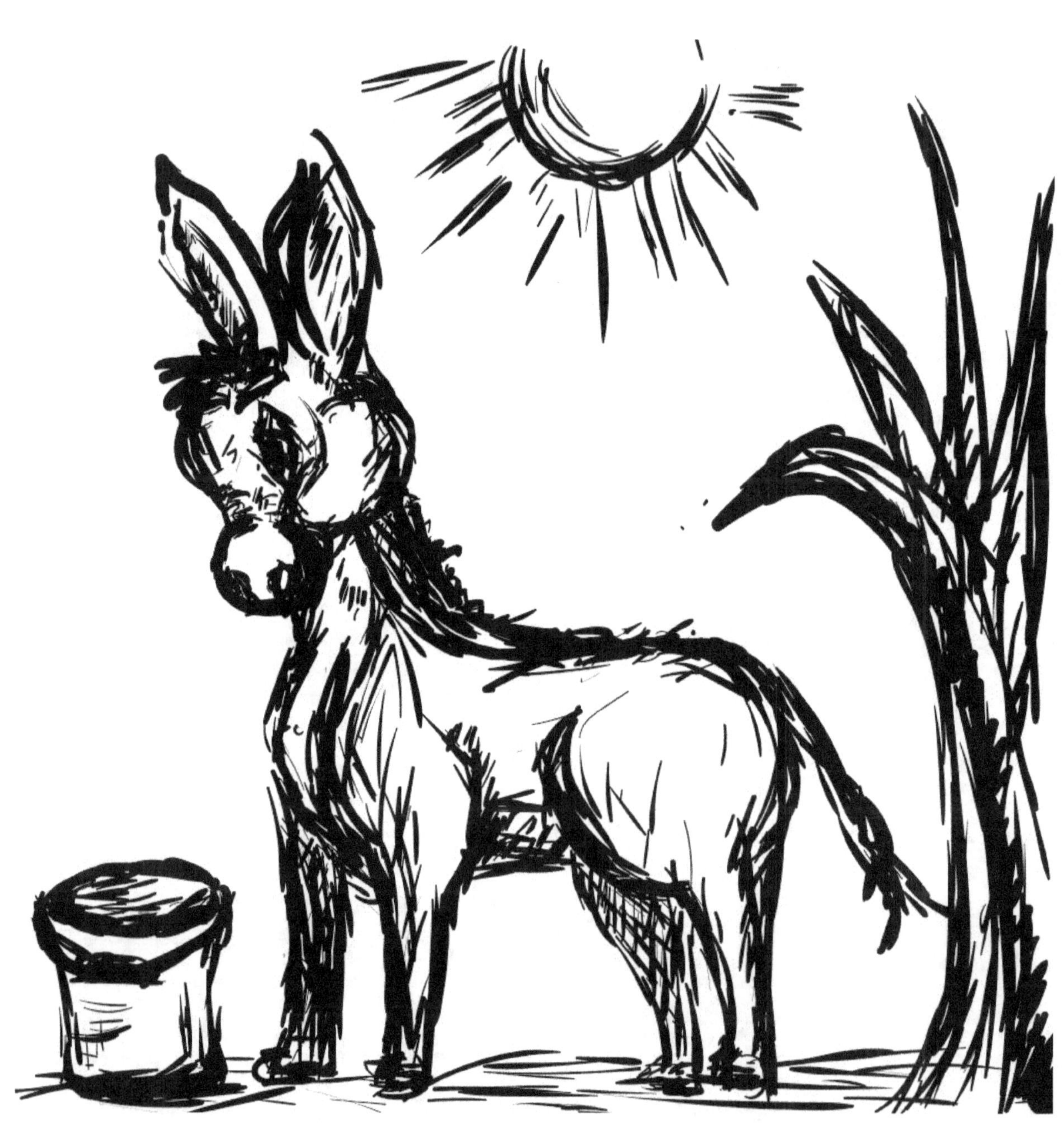

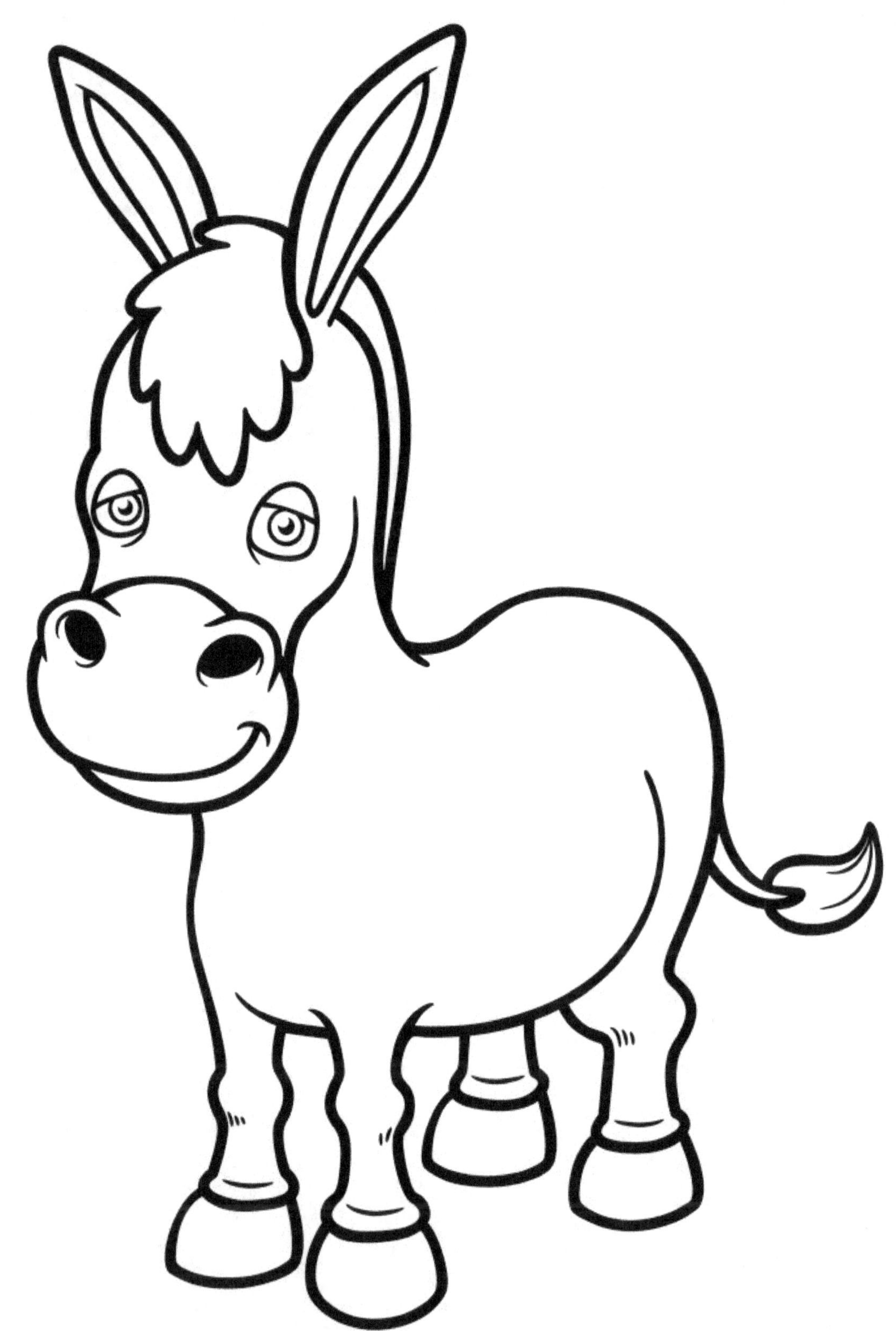

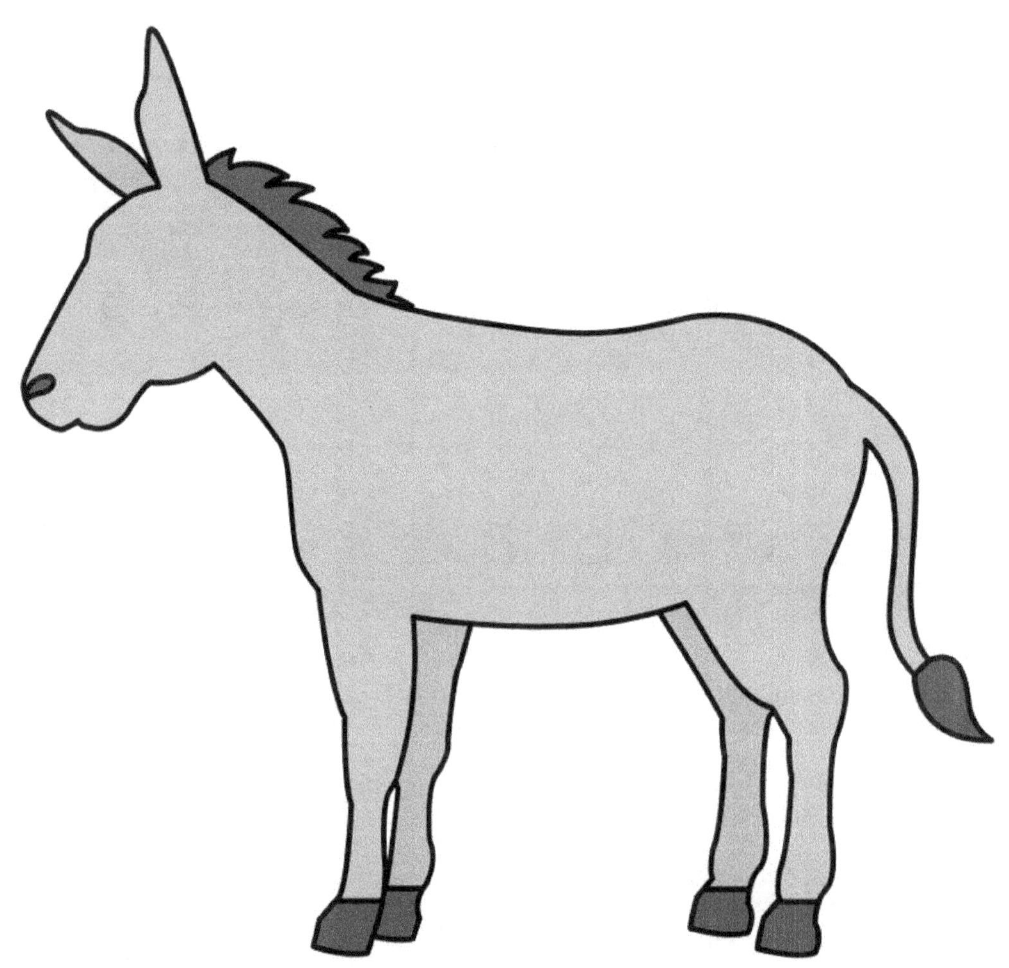

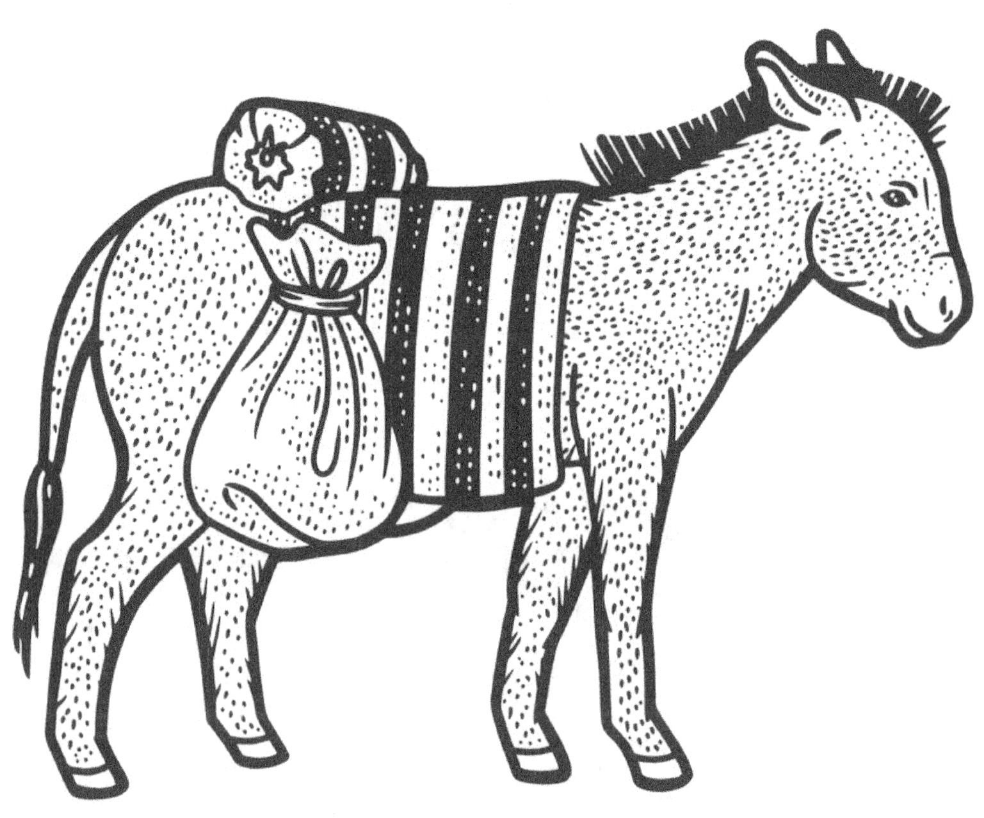

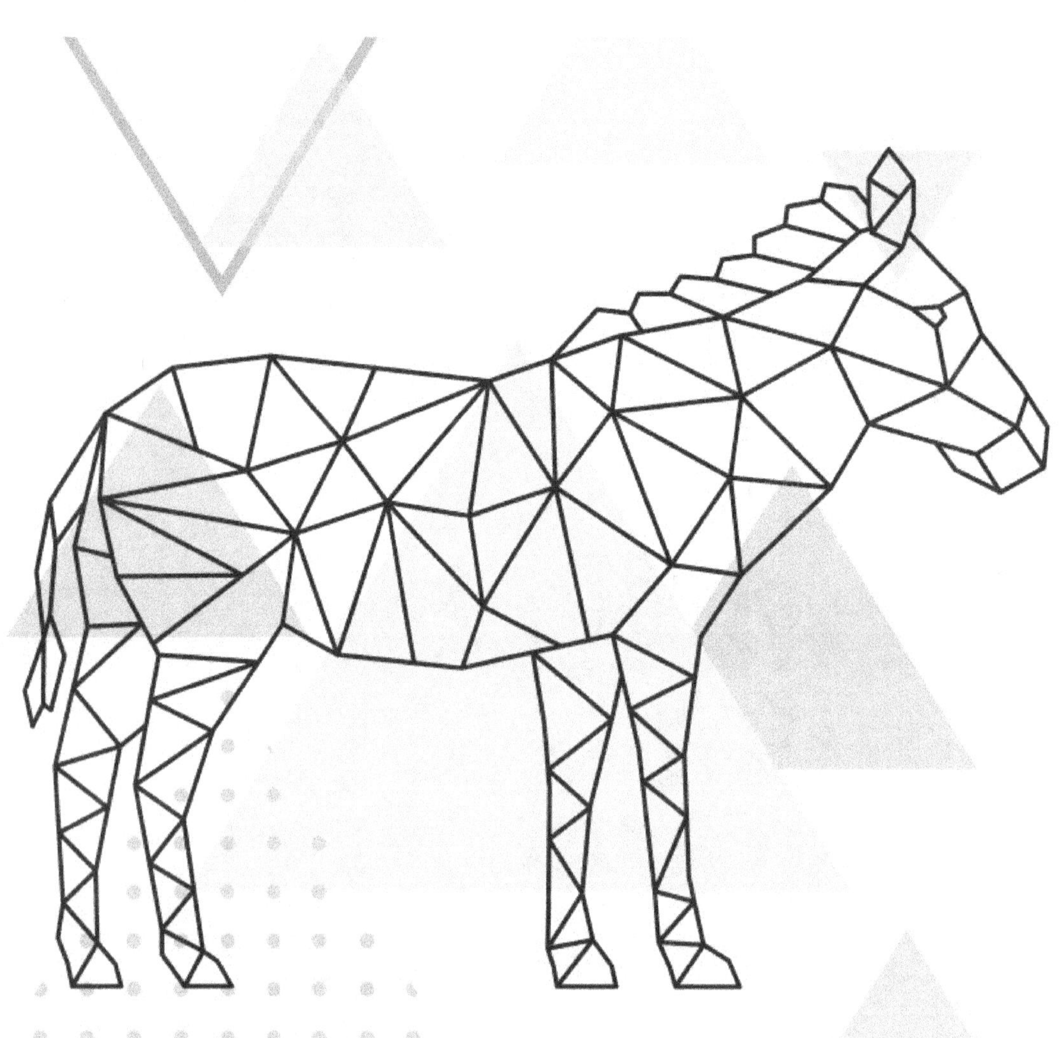

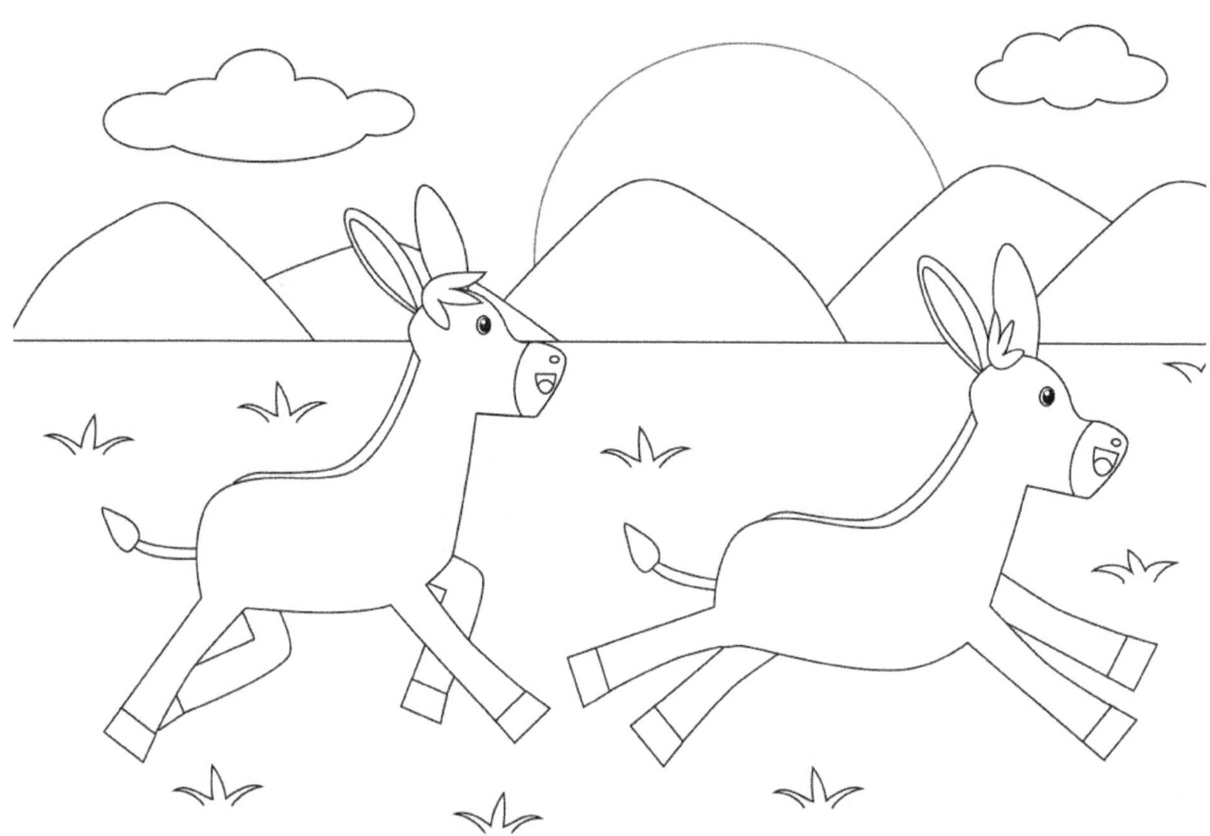

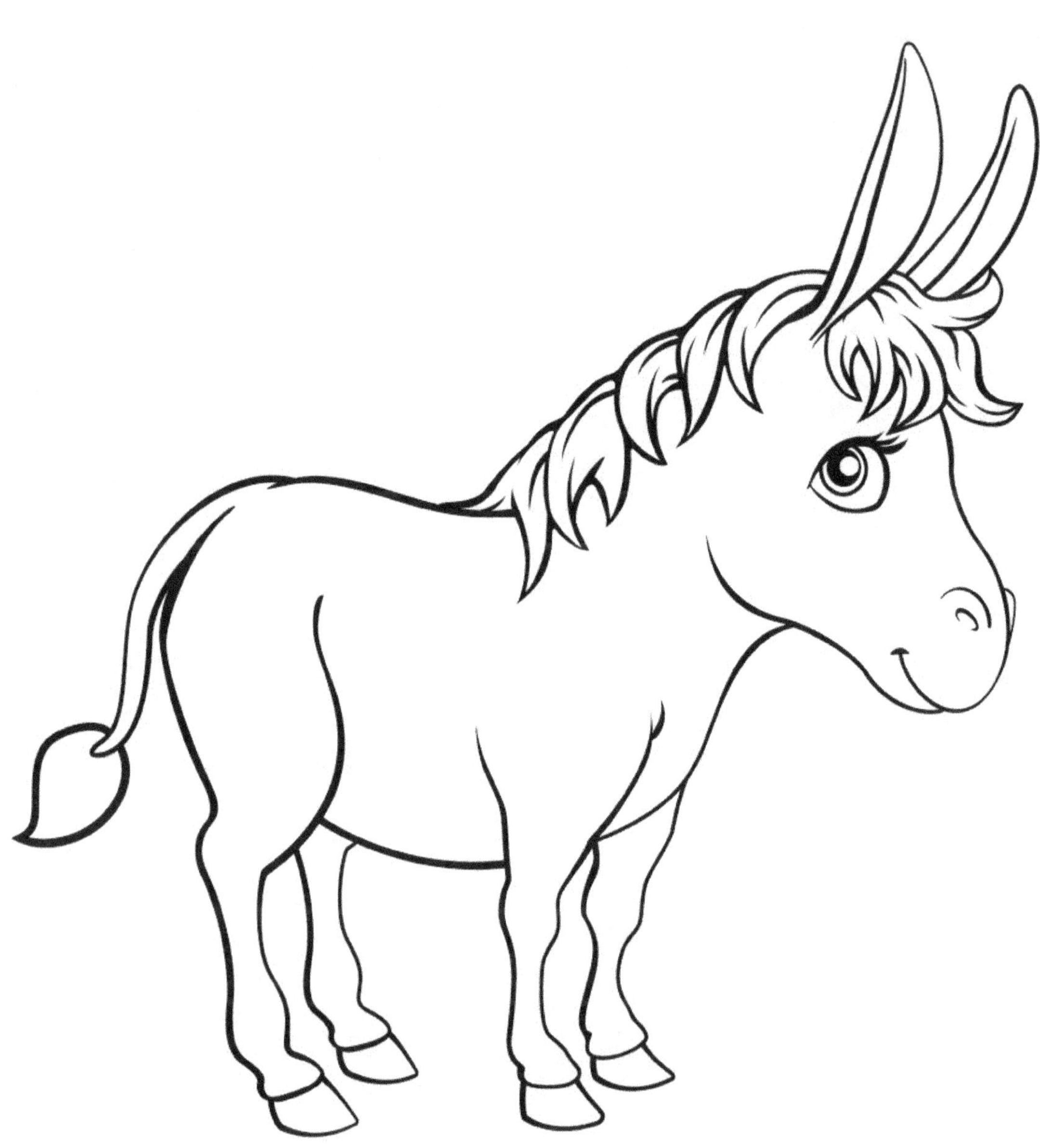

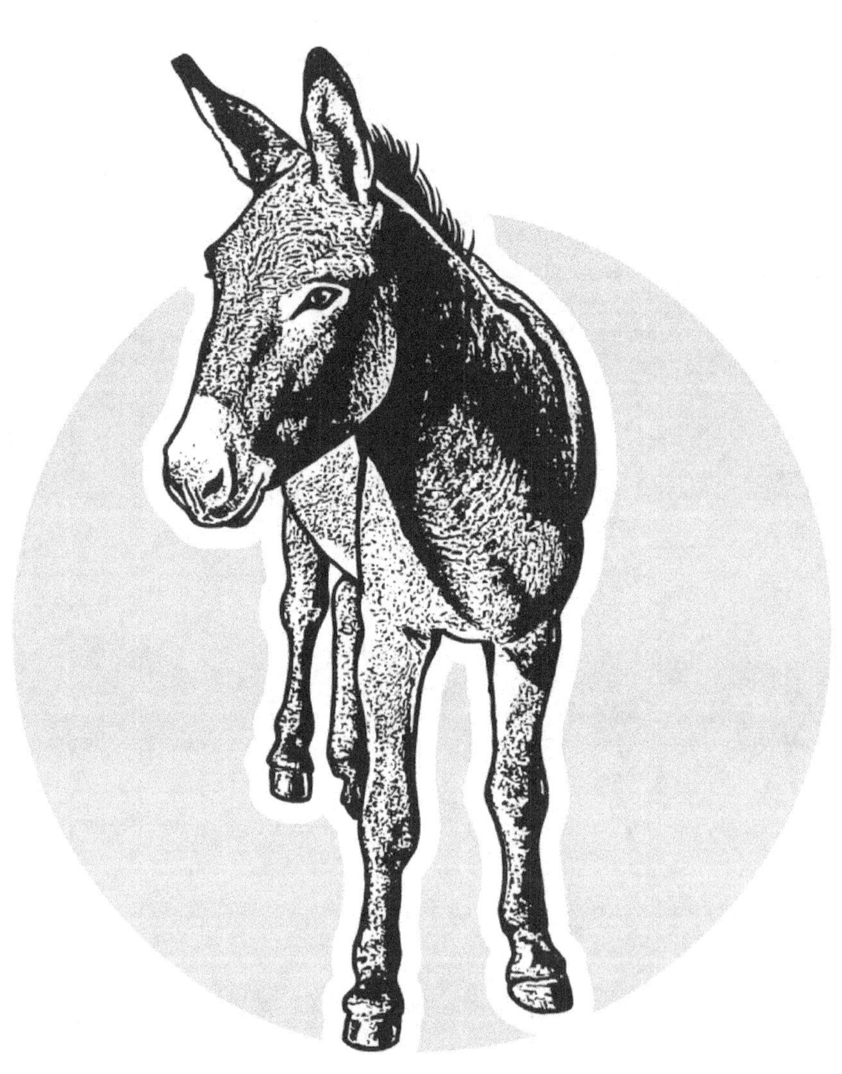

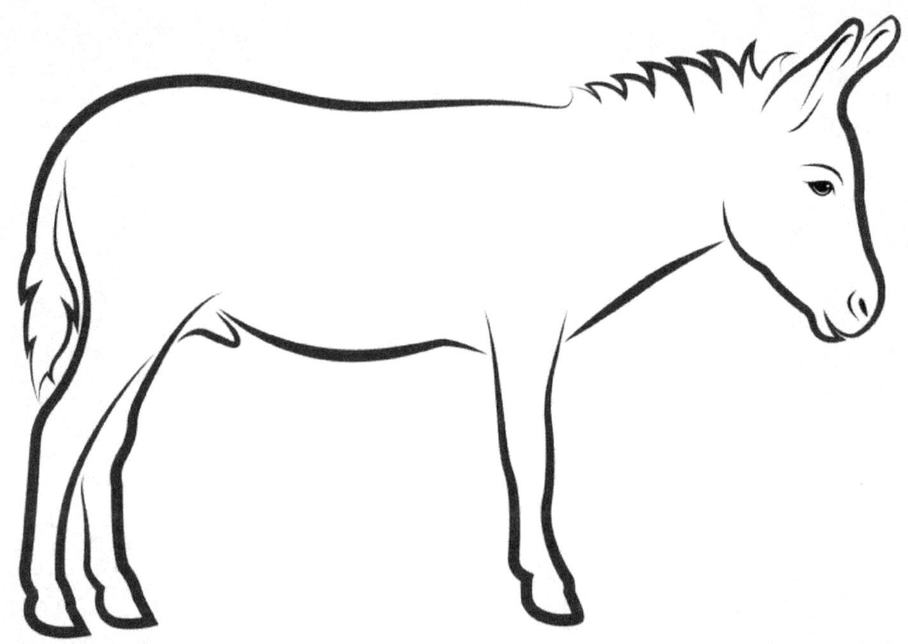

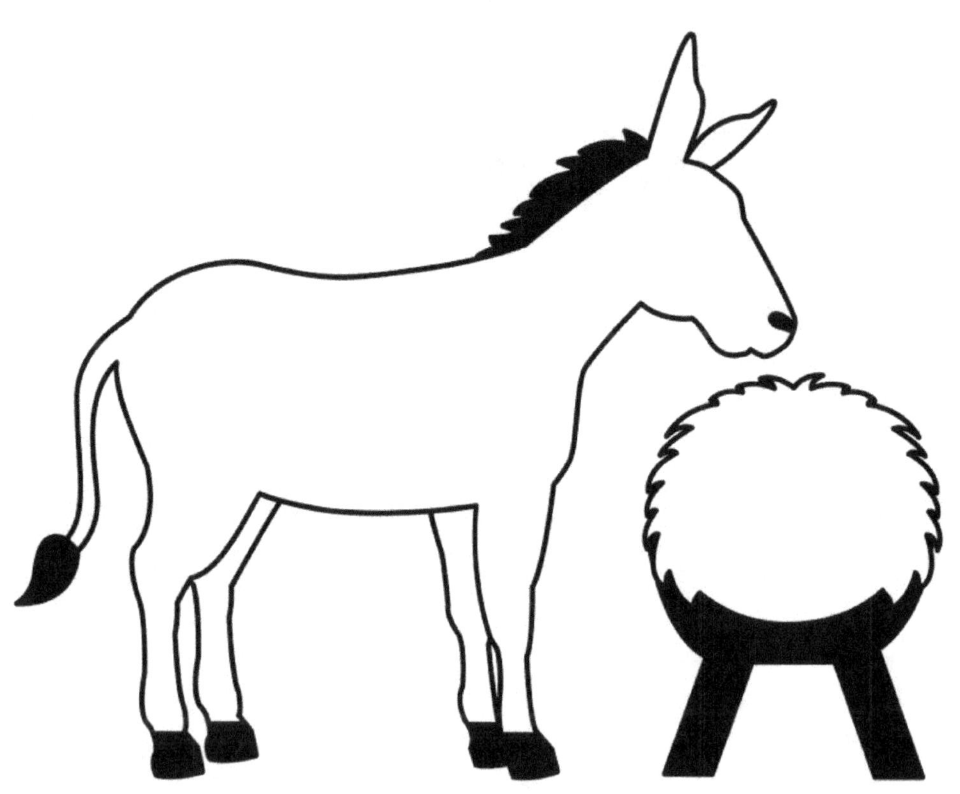

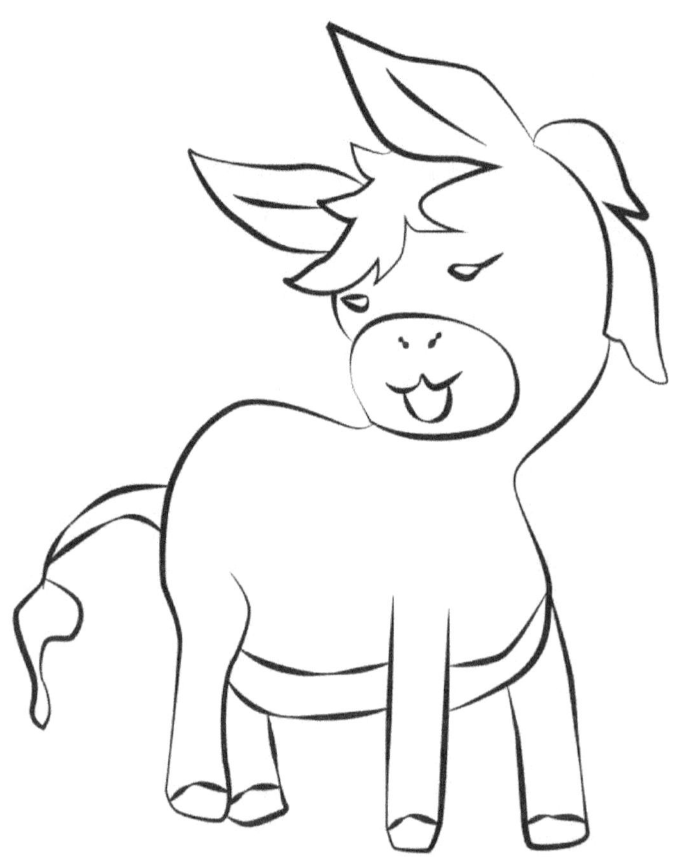

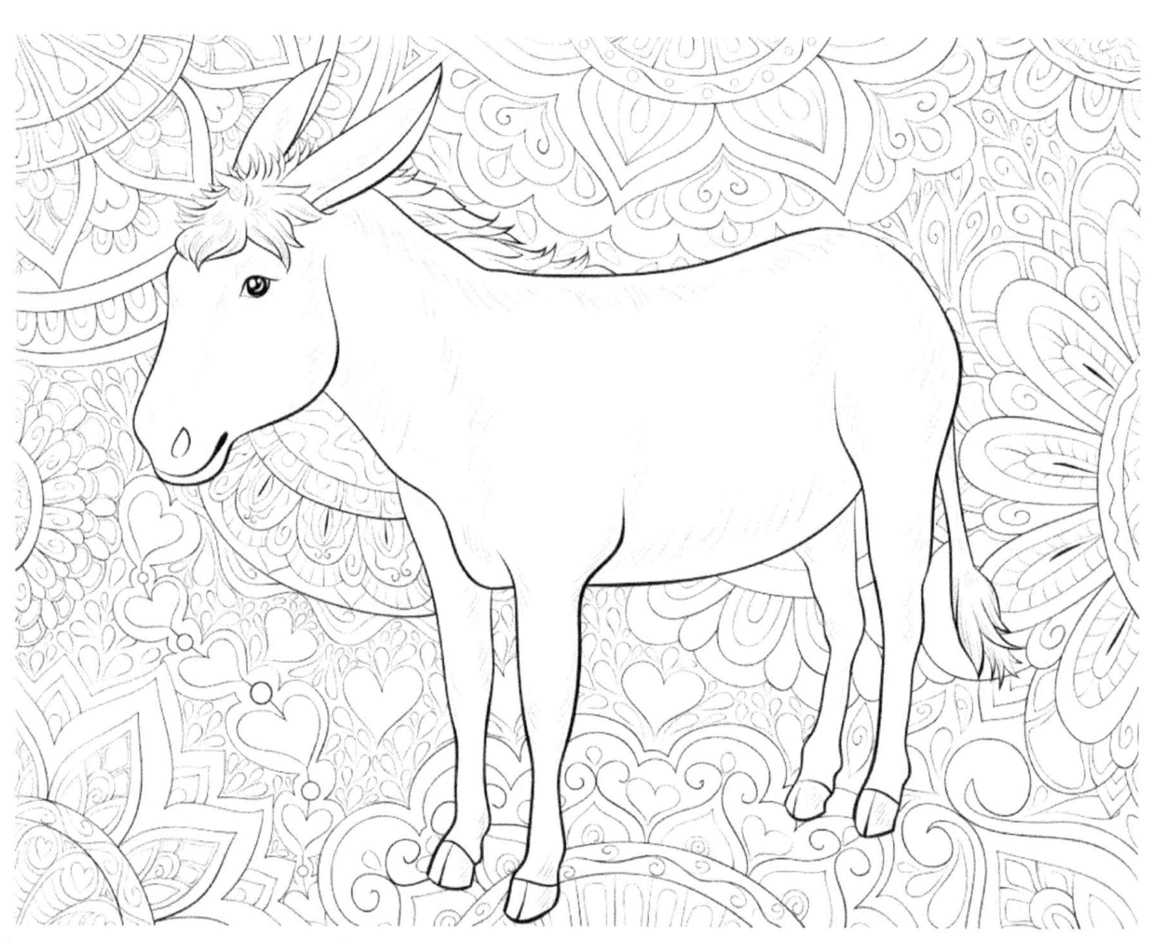

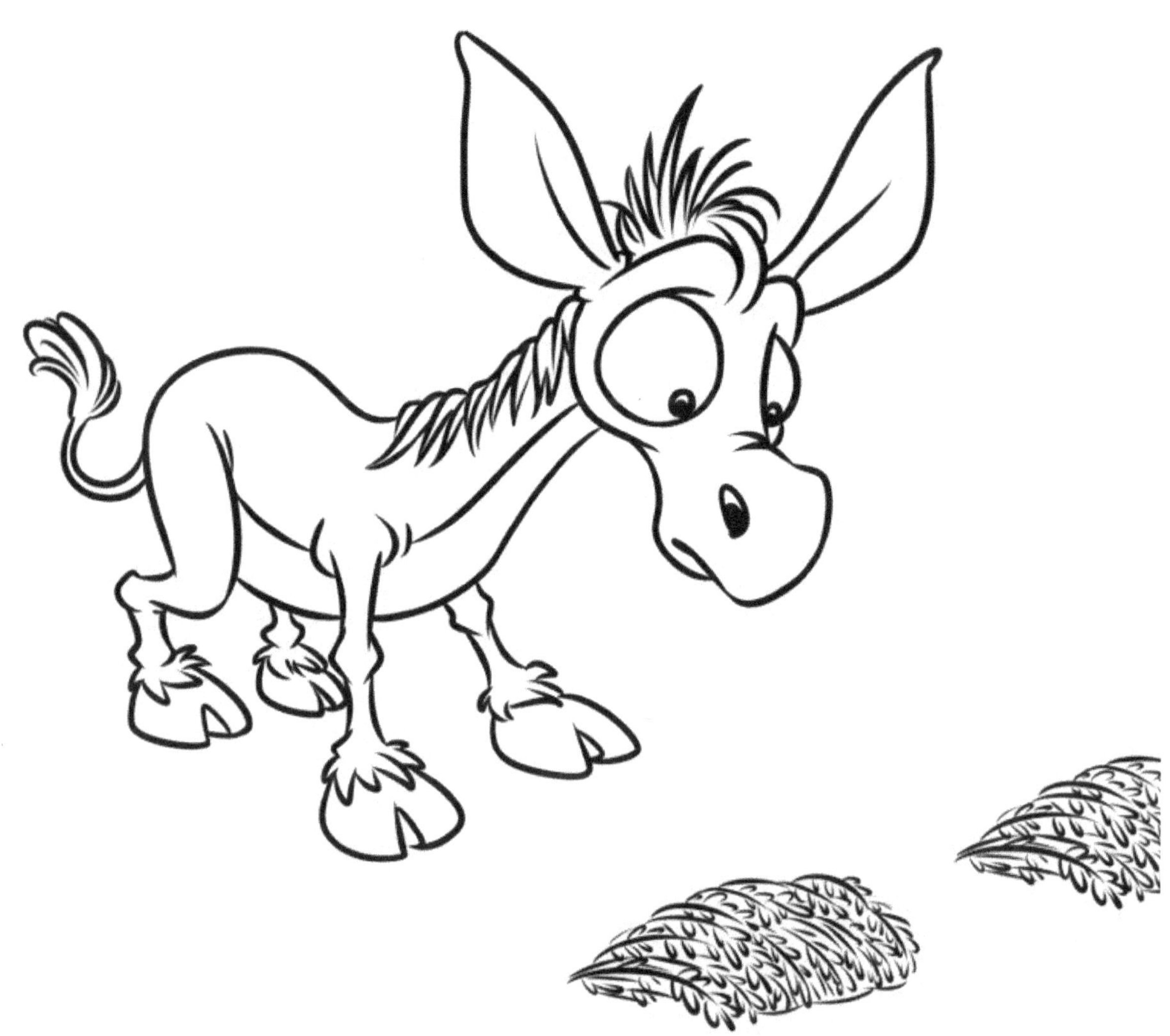

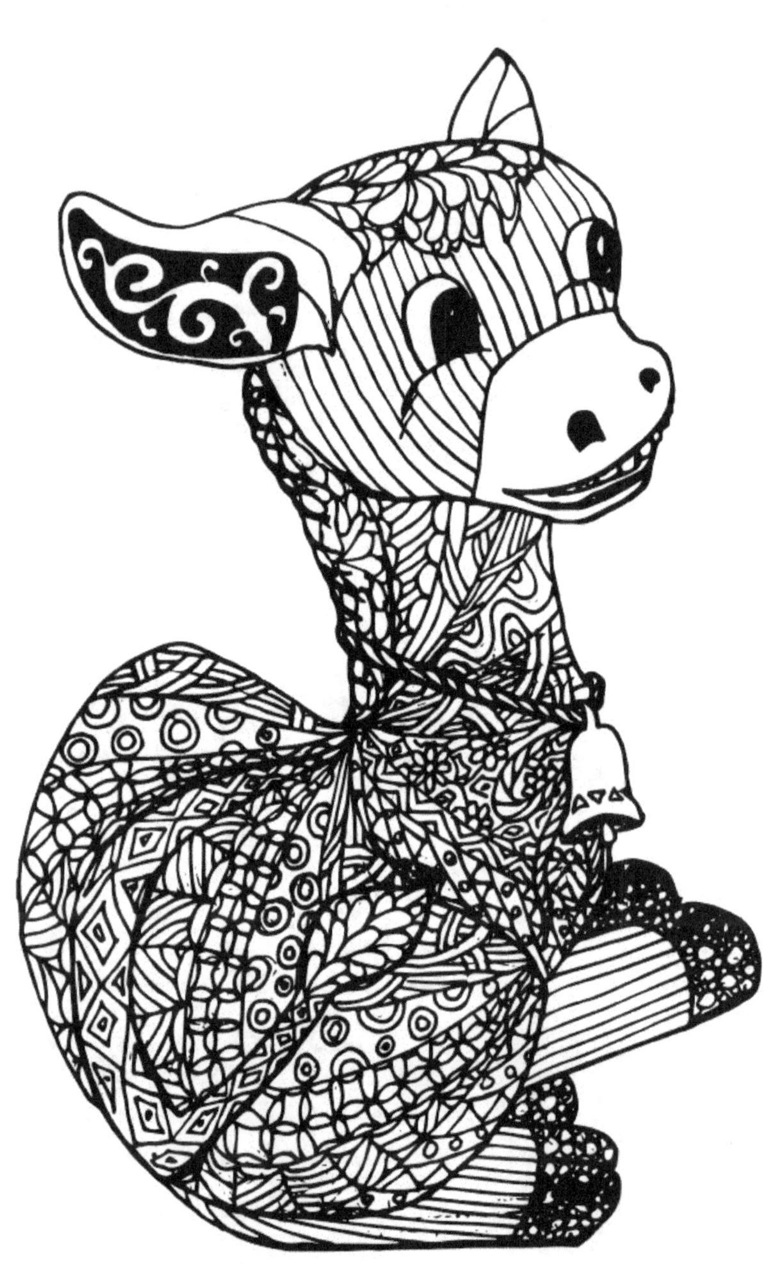

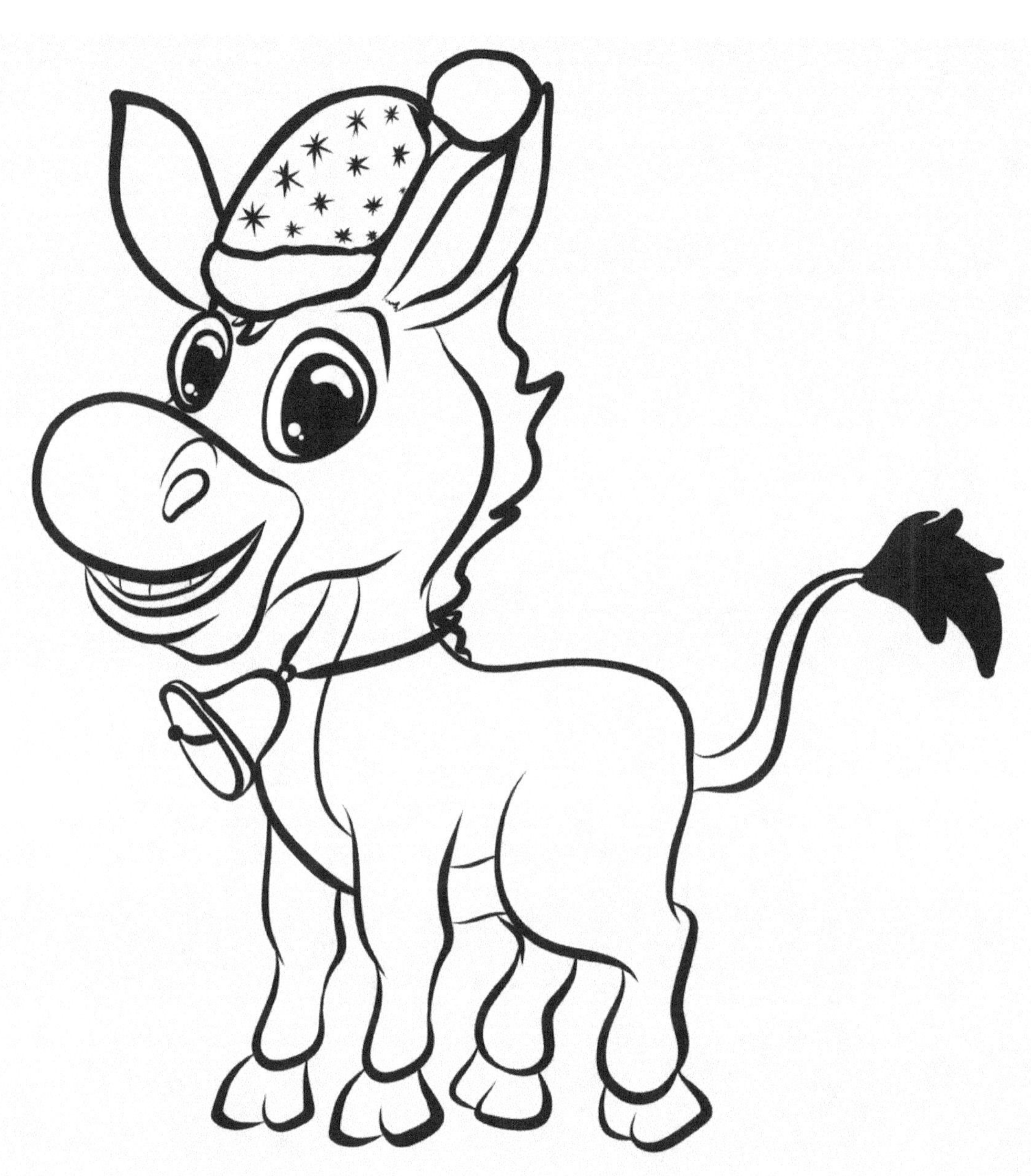

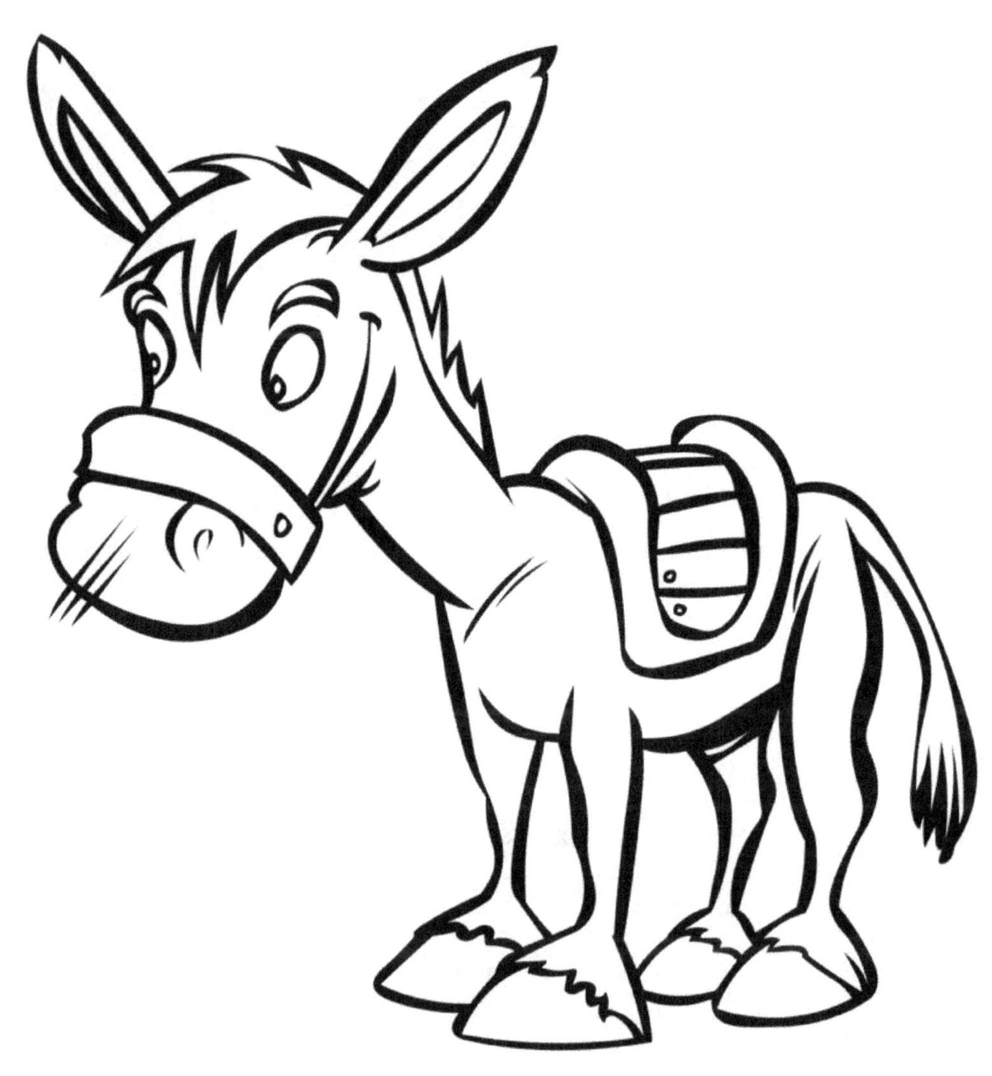